Xenophobe's®
guide to the
POLES

Ewa Lipniacka

D1488027

Xenophobe's Guides

Published by Xenophobe's® Guides
London SW9 7QH
United Kingdom

Telephone: +44 (0)20 7733 8585
E-mail: info@xenophobes.com
Web site: www.xenophobes.com

First printed 1994
New editions 2000, 2009, 2012
Reprinted/updated 1997, 1998, 2000, 2002,
2004, 2006, 2007, 2009, 2010, 2011, 2012,
2013

Editor – Catriona Tulloch Scott
Series Editor – Anne Tauté

Cover designer – Jim Wire & Vicki Towers
Printer – Polestar Wheatons, Devon

Cover: a Kraków crib (see page 60)

ePub ISBN: 9781908120724
Mobi ISBN: 9781908120731
Print ISBN: 9781906042448

Contents

'Geopolitics is the chief architect of the Polish character.'

The Polish population is 38 million compared with
9 million Swedes, 82 million Germans, 10 million Czechs,
5 million Slovaks, 10 million Hungarians, 44 million
Ukrainians, 4 million Lithuanians, 144 million Russians,
62 million British, and 315 million Americans.

Poland is 1½ times the size of Spain and a bit smaller
than Germany, but could fit into Russia 54 times.

Nationalism & Identity

Forewarned

Legend has it that one fine spring morning in ancient times, three Slavonic brothers, Czech, Lech, and Rus, set out to find new homes. Czech founded the Czech nation in the first good clearing they came to. The other two carried on until Lech saw an eagle building its nest, took it as a sign from the gods, and founded Gniezno, the first capital of Poland. Rus travelled on.

Lech's choice must rank with the ten worst decisions in history. Most of Poland is a flat open plain described by military experts as an 'ideal spot for a battlefield' (a feature exploited today by rental rather than invasion, for NATO manoeuvres, amongst others). Poland has been fought on or over at some time or another by virtually every country in Europe, including, amazing as it may seem, Sweden, and for whole centuries at a time it disappeared off the map altogether.

> **Most of Poland is a flat open plain described by military experts as an 'ideal spot for a battlefield'.**

But the past is another country. Today Poland is vibrantly independent and planning to stay that way. It's holding its own in the EU and is as keen on playing host to American rocket bases as it previously was to Russian ones. The only invasions it anticipates, or hopes for, are from tourists, and investors.

How the Poles see themselves

The Poles are self-critical; they know themselves inside out, warts and all. What is more, they will compulsively pick at their blemishes. There is not a problem, be it social, political, economic, national or local, which is not regularly and minutely dissected, put together again in every order imaginable and argued over endlessly. There is no national characteristic, either real or imagined, which has not been lamented, and its consequences listed. But when it comes to transferring the words into deeds – well, that is the trouble with Poles: argumentative, undisciplined, no follow-through, straw fire, as any Pole will tell you, interminably.

> **❝ The Poles are self-critical; they know themselves inside out, warts and all. What is more, they will compulsively pick at their blemishes. ❞**

However, this is a game only the home team can play. They would rather not have their faults pointed out by others. Under attack, they will defend every flaw, usually beginning with the phrase, 'But you couldn't possibly understand, the problem is so Polish.' Persist and you will offend and, with a Pole, taking offence comes only too easily, although luckily it doesn't last long. The most perfect solutions to all their problems more often than not are arrived at late at night, with alcohol fumes heating the air, but are forgotten with the hangover in the morning.

How they see others

Slavonic brotherhood notwithstanding, the Poles have always considered that East is East and West is best and the twain meet on Poland's eastern frontiers. If money talks, then what it tells the Poles is to travel west when seeking fame and fortune because to the east lie lands that are rich with people who are poor and who cannot afford Polish plumbers.

Their Russian neighbours are seen as brutish; a people born to be dominated, neither enterprising nor hard working, their successes being put down to sheer weight of numbers and ownership of essential raw materials. Although wary of the Russian mafia, on whom they lay the blame for the rise in their own crime rate, the Poles were quick to capitalise on the opportunities that trade with Russia and its former empire offered and many a fortune was made, and lost, on the tricky Russian market. Because of this familiarity, the Poles were the first to warn of the danger of Russia's stranglehold on world resources. Now, when Russians turn off the gas tap with every cold snap, the rest of Europe can more easily understand Polish fears and resentment.

> **If money talks, then what it tells the Poles is to travel west when seeking fame and fortune.**

The Poles find their other neighbours, the Germans, a dull lot who, left to their own devices, will stay in their own backyard and nurture *Heimat*, but as a nation (whether by war or trade) are born to dominate. Some Poles still worry that Germany might try to reclaim Silesia, but they hope that their interdependent economies and joint EU membership will keep German militancy at bay. An ever-increasing army of Polish migrants are making their home in Germany and 25% of Polish exports head there too.

> **The Poles are adept at dancing on tightropes.**

The Poles have the misfortune to be sandwiched between Germany and Russia and try to turn it to their advantage by playing business partner to either and middleman to both. But then, they're adept at dancing on tightropes.

For nations to admire, Poles look further afield. Most frequently, in search of style gurus, they turn to Italy, and not for the first time in history. Bona Sforza, wife of Zygmunt the Aged, introduced the Renaissance to Poland, along with architects, artists and craftsmen, and revolutionised Polish cuisine by bringing lettuce, leeks, cabbages and cauliflowers from Italy with her. In the 18th century, Bacciarelli and Canaletto painted Warsaw, which was being remodelled by, amongst others, Italian architect Dominic Merlini. After the Second World War, Canaletto's paintings were used as a guide for the reconstruction of streets and façades that the Germans had demolished.

For centuries the Poles, especially the aristocracy,

slavishly followed French style from language to fashion, and lived in France if they could afford it. Poles
who fought bitterly to save themselves from becoming
Russians or Germans voluntarily made themselves
imitation Frenchmen. Napoleon was revered, though
he only saw the Poles as can-
non fodder, and Polish law
and many civil institutions
are based on the Napoleonic
code. But French xenophobia
and frequent ganging up with
Germany in EU forums, has
brought the one-sided love
affair to an end. Relations are so frosty that even the
French language is rarely taught in Polish schools.

> **Nowadays it's the
English who have captured
Polish hearts and minds:
English pubs, English
products, the English
language taught
in all schools.**

Nowadays Polish hearts and minds belong to the
English. There are English pubs and English products,
signs in English over shop doors, and English taught
in all schools. Football fans even try to measure up to
English football hooligans, luckily without much success. Britain and Ireland were the first EU countries to
open their doors to the Poles, who flock there to
work, study and play. Consequently, Roman
Catholicism is the fastest growing religion in Britain
and European demographic statisticians are working
overtime to keep up.

Poles admire the Americans for their single-minded
pursuit of wealth, but see them as *nie kulturalni*

(uncultured) – a signal condemnation in Polish eyes. American 'Polish' jokes have little currency in Poland. However, Poles laugh at Polish Americans and see them as a naïve lot, but put this down to the effect of living in America.

For all that the Scandinavians are just across the Baltic and frequent ferries ply merrily between them, there seems to be little bonding of souls. Shoals of Poles go to Sweden and Norway to augment family finances by fruit picking and the like, and Swedish companies turn to Poland for cheap labour and designers – though Poles are shy about the former and the Swedes are loathe to admit to the latter. Only recently has the founder of IKEA admitted that his fortune (and fondness for vodka) came from sourcing his flatpacks in Poland in the 1960s. Not that any of this generates heat. A placid indifference reigns on both sides – a phenomenon amongst neighbours. They share the Baltic, but little else. Oil and water just don't mix.

> **Polish Poles see Polish Americans as a naïve lot, but put this down to the effect of living in America.**

With their smaller neighbours, political expediency is leading to a burial of the Polish/Ukrainian hatchet, while the Lithuanians are tolerated, in fact quite liked, although sadly the feeling is not always mutual: the two shared a government for too long, with the Poles as senior partner. With so many Poles earning their crust in the West, much of the employment slack in Poland is being taken up by Ukrainians and Lithuanians. The Czechs are considered too lacking in soul to be proper Slavs. The street cred they earned by choosing a playwright for president is spent. On the other hand, the Slovaks, with whom the Poles share the Tatra Mountains, are well liked. However, it is the Hungarians who the Poles treat as brothers, although they are not Slavs at all. Though they share neither border nor language, or possibly because of this, Hungarians are seen as kindred spirits, sharing aspirations, temperament and love of strong drink.

> **The Poles have always been seen as mad romantics. For this read 'manipulable hotheads' – all too often true.**

How others see them

The Poles have always been seen as mad romantics. For this read 'manipulable hotheads' – all too often true. Winston Churchill stated: 'There are few virtues that the Poles do not possess and few mistakes they have ever avoided.' Quentin Crisp went further by describing the Poles as: 'Not a nation, but an unsound state of mind.'

Much of the West sees the Poles as a workforce on the move, a nation of remittance men. The Hungarians admire the Poles for having retained their economic and political miracle, their own having hit the buffers. But being hero-worshipped doesn't come easy to a Pole as heroes don't complain, but you cannot be a good Pole without being able to indulge in a jolly good moan.

Before the Second World War, the Poles were considered to be 'Middle Europeans'. After the war, the country itself having shifted considerably westwards, Poles were known as 'East Europeans'. Since the fall of the Berlin Wall and the newly found independence of the Baltic States, Poland, without moving an inch, has become Central European again. It is hardly surprising, therefore, that many people have no idea where Poland is. Some confuse it with Holland. Many imagine it as permanently snow-bound, presumably associating it with the North Pole.

> **66 You cannot be a good Pole without being able to indulge in a jolly good moan. 99**

Character

The defensive Pole

Geopolitics is the chief architect of the Polish character. The Poles, famed as magnificent fighters, are in reality avid self-defenders. They would much rather not have to be. Even in its brief period of expansion in the 15th century, Poland acquired territory by treaty,

8

not battle, huddling together with Lithuania against the Teutonic Knights (Prussians by any other name).

Polish xenophobia is a self-defence mechanism: essential to the Poles' survival is the obsessive nurturing of language, culture and traditions, all of which are portable and can be handed on 'underground'.

Polish borders are a thing of such infinite fluidity that geography teachers are rumoured to have a special salary supplement for the extra hours of preparation they have to put in when establishing how many countries border with Poland at any given time, and which rivers are in or out. This also explains why more Poles live outside Poland's borders than inside. Many were left behind during border shifts – like the little old lady who, when informed that her home was now in Russia, not Poland, said, 'Thank God, I couldn't have stood another of those cold Polish winters.'

> **Polish borders are a thing of such infinite fluidity that geography teachers are rumoured to have a special salary supplement for the extra hours of preparation they have to put in.**

Some were reluctant tourists, a long-standing favourite trip being 'Siberia by cattle truck'. Some were washed out by the tides of uprisings or war and deposited wherever. For example, the Poles in France are relics of the 19th-century uprisings, while the Poles in Britain were stranded after the Second World War, hence the Ealing or Bradford Poles.

Now that the Soviet Union is no more, Polish communities have emerged from all its former territories as far afield as Kazakhstan, and former Polish towns like Lviv in the Ukraine and Vilnius in Lithuania.

> **Exiles from all over the world flock to Poland, delighted that all those Saturday mornings spent learning Polish are paying off at last.**

Poland has ever been a net provider of economic migrants and many made for the Statue of Liberty along with every other hungry European. The biggest urban concentration of Poles today, after Warsaw, is in Chicago. There are sizeable Polish communities in Germany, Brazil, Peru, anywhere – in fact, you can't travel far in the world without bumping into a Pole. This means that today's Polish citizens are inveterate travellers, not on package tours but on family visits. Exiles from all over the world, even unto the third generation, flock to and from Poland bent on business and pleasure, delighted that all those Saturday mornings spent learning Polish are paying off at last.

Regional differences in Poland are often still dictated by the national characteristics of the 18th- and 19th-century occupants of the region. Hence Poznań, once ruled by the Prussians, is home to a law-abiding and industrious people, fanatically tidy and too pedantic for words who, infuriatingly, always turn up everywhere on time. Kraków and its environs are full of petty bureaucrats, like their old Austrian masters. And in Warsaw and district you will find sloppy layabouts, quite like the Russians, in fact.

The regional minority held dear by all Poles, and butt of affectionate 'straw-chewing yokel' jokes, are the Górale, the inhabitants of the mountain regions. The story is told of the Góral who, watching a townie doing his morning press-ups in front of his tent, declared that he had never before known a wind so strong that it blew a woman from under her mate.

The flexible Pole

It is not surprising that key national characteristics are adaptability, a knack for improvisation, and the ability to make the best of what is available. A good Polish cook is one who can make gourmet soup from a rusty nail. Older Polish cook books give recipes of the

> **66 A good Polish cook is one who can make gourmet soup from a rusty nail. 99**

familiar 'take a dozen eggs' variety, alongside those for 'what to use if you have no...'. For example, 'Almond cake if you have no almonds (use ground beans and almond flavouring)'.

Although the economic imperative for these characteristics, known collectively in Polish as '*kombinowanie*', has gone, relegated to the history books along with the queues and shortages that gave birth to it, it is still an integral part of the Polish personality. A heady mix of cerebral gymnastics, technical skill, gung-ho can-do-ery and a pinch of deviousness, it enabled the Poles to rig up clever devices when there was nothing suitable on the market. It also showed them how to circumnavigate the unworkable regulations and laws that Communist governments created to confound their citizens. You might think these tactics would fade without the necessity to keep them honed. Not a bit of it. Poles now employ all their stratagems on the EU.

Poles apart

The Poles are either positive or negative. They work or they play. They are useless at the sort of playing at work that passes for industriousness in many Western European offices.

At the moment, Poles are divided between those who want to embrace the West, with everything that brings and entails, and those who would defend to the death the essential purity of Polishness (whatever that may be); those who feel that the Church should have a big say in government and those who think it should have none. The quintessential Polish dilemma is that two opposing views can be held simultaneously in one and

66 The quintessential Polish dilemma is that two opposing views can be held simultaneously in one and the same Polish breast. 99

the same Polish breast. They are either bubbling with life, or comatose; they love or they loathe. It is this total commitment to the occupation of the moment that earns them the reputation of being mercurial. As Hemar wrote in his song: 'If only Poles did systematically and economically what they do spontaneously, they would be perfect.'

The public Pole

Polish people are very public spirited. They consider it a moral duty to pass comment loud and clear on any-thing of which they may approve or disapprove. Thus, if you are in a public office tangling with bureaucracy (par for the course, as tangling is what Polish bureaucracy is

> **Poles consider it a moral duty to pass comment loud and clear on anything of which they may approve or disapprove.**

for), you will have a chorus of support from all other members of the queue. If you dawdle at a shop counter, you may have to endure comments on your ineptitude, lack of sense, morals, taste, and so on, from the folk behind you. Public officials and shop assistants will join in, on one side or the other, depending on their mood.

Any minor disaster that may befall you in public will be treated as street entertainment by the audience that will gather instantly. Exhibitionists, this is the nation for you. There is good reason, too, for the thick net curtains that adorn windows. It is an attempt to maintain some semblance of privacy. But it is a vain attempt. There is no defence against intrusion. In Poland, you need some form of light relief during the long winter nights, so you might as well give in and join the gossip circuit. It is the only chance you may have to correct a few of the wilder assumptions about your blameless life. It also means you always have a shoulder to cry on without the need to explain: people will know before you do what you are crying about.

> **In Poland, you need some form of light relief during the long winter nights, so you might as well give in and join the gossip circuit.**

Style

All – well, most – Poles are born with a sense of style. Even when resources are scant or non-existent, Poles manage to look stylish. This was most evident in the 1960s, when Warsaw shops were full of utility clothing yet the streets were thronged with a fashion parade to rival Carnaby Street or Montmartre. Only the right labels were missing, because the outfits had been run up on the home treadle sewing machine.

During the Second World War, in Palestine, Polish officers who had escaped from occupied Poland were incorporated into the British Army. Within days, they were transforming the standard issue British Army tropical baggy shorts into natty little bum-hugging numbers.

Devotion to style pervades all areas of life: the table might be rickety, but it is covered with a snowy table-cloth and decorated with a vase of flowers. The very first periodicals off the starting blocks in capitalist Poland were the style magazines: in fashion, in the garden, in the home. They thrived then and they are thriving still. These days Polish names can be spotted throughout the international style industry, from Ewa Lewis to Tomasz Starzewski.

The supreme example of Polish style is the stylish gesture. Who else would start a revolution with a logo? '*Solidarność*' (Solidarity) is a logo so success-ful that it ranks alongside Coca-Cola and Kellogg's for instant recognition worldwide, and with a style so convincing that it swept Mrs Thatcher, supreme hater of trades unions, into supporting one. Yet not a penny was spent on promoting it.

And on a personal level, just when you are most exasperated with a Pole for yet another promise unful-filled, a deadline unmet, a late arrival, or sheer thought-lessness, you will be disarmed by a stylish apology: an unexpected, perfectly judged gift and a nosegay of melting charm. How can you not forgive?

Beliefs & Values

Wealth

Poles didn't used to hunger for wealth and status because, under Communism, neither was possible or even permissible without a major compromise of personal values; and even before that any self-respecting Pole avoided 'trade'. The Polish economic miracle has astonished the world, but not as much as it has surprised the Poles themselves. Though most of the world acknowledges that Polish bankers were among the few responsible ones who did not gamble away the monies of their clients and country, the Poles themselves do not believe it and view every sign of economic downturn in the country (inevitable in a recession) as proof.

> **The Polish economic miracle has astonished the world, but not as much as it has surprised the Poles themselves.**

Yet perhaps Polish adeptness at economic realism is not so surprising. Poles have always had to get by and horse-trade. During Communism, especially its last stages, most economic exchange inside or outside the country was reduced to barter and invention. It was all valuable training. As the last few years have proved, being duff at business was not so much a national characteristic as a national inferiority complex.

The Polish businessman has always had to make his presence felt and remembered, despite his unpronounceable name. This may explain why Polish business cards are miniature works of art and, after the name, list every academic or other qualification, affiliation to institutions, marital status, shoe size, hat size... Business cards are handed out by all and sundry to all and sundry from a seemingly endless supply. You can be sure that the delegate still dishing out cards on the last day of a conference, when everybody else's supply is spent, is a Pole.

Status

Historically Poles were either gentry, and mostly impoverished, or peasants (there was no official middle ground). In many cases, the only distinction between the two was a gentrifying coat of arms.

Poland has never bestowed titles of honour on its citizens. All counts, princes and lords have been so honoured by other nation. Instead, liberal use is made of academic or professional titles, in conjunction with *Pan* (Mr) or *Pani* (Ms). If you admit to belonging to the medical profession, you will be addressed as 'Pan Doktór', or 'Pan Profesor' if you are an academic. 'Pan Profesor Doktór' is not uncommon, along with other amalgams even more absurd. You could even be called 'Pan Inżynier' if you inadvertently put B.Sc. after your name. ('Inżynier' –

> **❝ The title 'Engineer' means you have a university degree, not that you have come about the boiler. ❞**

17

Engineer – indicates that you have a university degree, and not that you have come about the boiler.)

The habit of most invaders of lining up intellectuals against a wall and shooting them makes it surprising that anyone still wants to be one. But Poles do, in droves. So, if you know it, flaunt it. Everyone in Poland loves a know-all and specialists of whatever variety are lionised.

> **66 Everyone in Poland loves a know-all and specialists of whatever variety are lionised. 99**

The way to obviate the pitfalls of formal v. informal address (the 'you/thou' problem) is to drink a *Bruderschaft* – a procedure you approach only after you have downed at least half a bottle with the partner you are bruding your shaft with. You sit opposite each other, as for arm wrestling, with a glass in your right hand, you cross arms, and then try to get the contents of the glass into your mouth rather than down your front. The passion of the kiss which usually follows is a matter of the taste of at least one of the participants.

Hospitality

The old Polish tenet of 'A guest in the home: God in the home' still holds good, and most Poles view hospitality as a sacred obligation. Given the acres of still uninhabited terrain and the weather, this is probably a good thing. However, more recent cynical versions

18

such as 'A guest in the home: a pregnant wife', or 'A guest in the home: God knows what for', might be an indication that it is all wearing a bit thin.

Another tenet, still observed, is, 'Get into debt, but be a good host', which can be a source of bewilderment for guests. Even in times of shortages or hardship, Poles laid a table that had visitors disbelieving reported economic realities. Polish hospitality has a way of leaving guests with an embarrassment of *richesses*, and hosts eating up leftovers for a week. When Poles cater, they cater for a battalion.

Courtship and marriage

Polish men and boys (including small ones) still kiss women's hands. This can be, but isn't necessarily, an integral part of flirting. They also hold doors open, light cigarettes, carry bags and generally behave in a way that we are told the English gentleman behaved before the feminists got to him. It is, of course, Polish women who

> **66 Polish men and boys (including small ones) still kiss women's hands. 99**

ensure their men remain gentlemen, by the scruff of the neck if necessary. Polish New Man must wash dishes and push the pram.

The men may flirt outrageously, but not in the florid, poetic, but sadly unconvincing manner of the Latin. Your eyes won't be compared to diamonds, but your new hairstyle or weight-loss will be noticed, your new outfit admired. You will believe him and feel wonderful – yet beware. He might still respect you in the morning, but he will poodle off home to his wife or mother all the same.

The women are just as skilled at flirting; in fact, both sexes, young and old, consider it an art.

Most Poles end up marrying other Poles, and most remain monogamous. In cafés and restaurants, for reasons that remain obscure, couples tend to sit side by side, not opposite each other as in Britain. Most Poles can dance – tangos, foxtrots and waltzes – and do so cheek to cheek, with real steps, not vague swaying shuffles, even at discos.

> **To be addressed as 'little fish' or 'little frog' should not be a cause for concern.**

To be addressed as 'little fish' or 'little frog' should not be cause for concern. These are well-established terms of endearment, and mean your partner loves you dearly, but cannot pronounce, or has temporarily forgotten, your name.

Should he or she take you home to meet mother, size up the family carefully. If you decide to settle in Poland, beware. Intensive building has eased the housing shortage but it has been replaced with astronomical increases in the price of property, so you might be living with them for a long time, as might your children and their spouses. By then, the older brothers and sisters and their families might have found accommodation of their own, and one of them might have taken grandma – but don't count on it. The divorce rate is one of the lowest in Europe, but this may be because many divorced couples still have to live together.

Behaviour

The family

The Poles extend their families like elastic. Cousins are frequently called brothers and sisters, and being 'cousins' can encompass a broad spectrum of relationships. Such relationships not only mean more people at table, they mean obligations if needs arise, in both directions: favours given and received. A careful eye is kept on the well-being of other family members in case they can be tapped for something.

> **A careful eye is kept on the well-being of other family members in case they can be tapped for something.**

If, on meeting, you are told that 'You look well', especially by someone of your own sex, check the bathroom scales. This is the code for 'You have put on weight'. The obverse, 'You don't look well', meaning 'You've lost weight', is usually only said by those of a wider girth who are simply jealous, or by mothers.

Polish mothers view all humanity in the same way the residents of Strasbourg view geese – there for the fattening. If a Polish mother tells you she has a problem child, it does not mean little Tomek has burnt his school to the ground and is being sought by the police of five counties. It means he won't eat his dinner.

The elderly

Changing times and galloping inflation were unkind to the Polish pensioner, but a spate of church supported, right-wing minority and coalition governments has rediscovered and re-empowered grannies (collectively known as 'mohair berets') and pensions have improved, unlike unemployment pay which ceases after six months. It is now granny who is subsidising and even, in dire cases, supporting the extended family. Even in affluent families, it is customary for grandparents to bring up the youngest generation.

> **If you are a cantankerous old person, Poland is the place for you.**

Respect for the elderly is as strong as ever. If you are a cantankerous old person, Poland is the place for you. You can loudly criticise any youngster foolish enough to stand near you, whether related to you or not. You have priority everywhere, as of right. You can prod the most obnoxious-looking punk on the bus with finger or umbrella, and he will vacate his place without a murmur. The pregnant, and those festooned with children, will do likewise. If you are too shy to prod, just look sufficiently old and helpless, and fellow passengers will prod on your behalf, accompanied by a chorus from every other senior citizen in sight.

Children

Not mothers, but mother-in-laws are expected to bring up children (especially those whose parents are abroad), and often run the households of their working children. The Poles love children, especially babies, take them everywhere and spoil them so much that it is surprising how well behaved most of them are. Few children are sent away to boarding school, although most are sent to camp with the scouts or other youth organisations, or to relatives in the country, to give them a chance to run wild during summer holidays.

> **66 The Poles love children and spoil them so much that it is surprising how well behaved most of them are. 99**

Parties are family affairs, encompassing everyone from Great-Aunt Josephine to the smallest infant. Even childless adults have the young underfoot so often that they know how to deal with them, and children quickly learn just how far they can push the adults and get away with it.

Animals

Given the unbelievably cramped living conditions that still prevail in the tower blocks, it is hard to understand why urban Poles choose Alsatians and Dobermans as pets and not Chihuahuas, or why they have pets at all. The general rule seems to be: the smaller the flat, the larger the dog, with the exception of Kraków where citizens keep miniature dogs – but this is attributed to their legendary meanness.

> **66 Citizens of Kraków keep miniature dogs, but this is attributed to their legendary meanness. 99**

In rural areas, however, pets work for a living and keep rodents down and intruders out (depending on the species), or they are out of job, house and home. Other animals are safer in Poland than elsewhere. The Bieszczady forest on the eastern borders is home to primeval trees and exceptional wild-life (including bison and wild boar). Almost a quarter of the world's stork population nests on Polish trees, roofs and telegraph poles, which means that every fourth stork is a Pole.

Manners

Stylish manners are a matter of course. Offering seats, opening doors – all are done with a flourish, though much of this is making an art form of a necessity, for woe betide the Pole who falls below the standard of behaviour decreed by the most vocal custodian of public morality in the world: the Polish grandmother.

Polish grandmothers have taken upon themselves a heavy burden: they have to ensure that their grandchildren, their neighbours' children, indeed the children of the nation – of whatever age – sit up straight and pass the salt just so. All this while simultaneously spoiling them rotten.

Children stay out of grandmother's way whenever they plan to infringe the morality code. Luckily, grandmothers were young once too. The priest listening to a string of men's names listed by a quavering voice from the confessional was finally stung to ask 'But how old are you, granny?' 'Eighty-three.' 'And you still carry on like that?' 'No, but it's so nice to remember.'

In winter you are expected to remove your snow-laden shoes before entering the house. There is usually a row of slippers by the front door, but since they are rarely of a size to fit your feet, Poles remember to put on clean, holeless socks when going visiting. Most homes have parquet floors to keep people in training for the harsh, icy, slippery winters. Museums and galleries refine this talent by insisting that you wear felt slippers over your shoes to protect the parquet floor (and polish it at the same time). The sensible prospective visitor to Poland puts in a few hours at the local ice-rink before setting out.

> **Most homes have parquet floors to keep people in training for the harsh, icy, slippery winters.**

25

Greetings

The Poles are very tactile, and kiss and hug at every opportunity. The standard greeting for those of either sex who are more than casual acquaintances is the bear-hug, followed by a touching of cheeks, and three air-kisses per person greeted.

For acquaintances of a lesser order, the handshake suffices but is obligatory. Everyone shakes hands with everyone, and progress along any high street is impeded by batches of greeters. Lounging teenagers have a strange, sideways, arm-outstretched, 'I'm being very laid back here, you understand' handshake. Solemn small boys make it look like the initiation rite to the Black-Hand Gang.

> **66 Never shake hands with a Pole as you cross a threshold – it is thought to bring bad luck to both parties and the house. 99**

Always remember to build handshaking time into meetings. A group of ten newcomers meeting a group of ten locals builds up to a lot of handshakes, and before you know it, it's time to go home.

Never shake hands with a Pole as you cross a threshold – it is thought to bring bad luck to both parties and to the house. Bemused non-Polish guests find themselves unceremoniously hauled in by the outstretched arm with shouts of 'Not over the threshold', their coats and shoes whisked off, then being bear-hugged and kissed three times and their stockinged or slippered feet tucked under the dining room table before they can manage to say 'I've come to read the meter'. The symbolic reason for this is lost in the mists of time, but the probable cause is the cold draughts that whistle round the region, and the outrageous cost of central heating.

Leisure & Pleasure

Staying in

From having the most politically repressed, dire television in the world, Poland has progressed to having the most liberal, dire television in the world. However, viewers can hop between four public, one religious, many local and countless commercial channels, the religious channel having the best reception, boosted as it is by a network of aerials on church spires).

'Commercial' equates to 'subscription' and the Poles do subscribe. Satellite dishes sprout from every roof.

When foreign programmes and films are shown, they are

> **The religious television channel has the best reception, boosted as it is by a network of aerials on church spires.**

neither dubbed nor sub-titled but translated simultaneously in an excited semi-whisper. In addition, the original sound track is not turned off, merely down: a conversation going on in the background which viewers try to keep up with in vain.

Polish news bulletins are read at breakneck speed as if newscasters were being paid by the word. The tone is more cosy than authoritative, almost like listening to remarkably well-informed neighbours gossiping. One sociologist called them 'soap operas for men'. Coverage is comprehensive, from all parts of the country and abroad. They are justifiably popular and regularly top the viewing charts. The public channels are deemed to be the more creditable. The logic for the order of items, the length of time devoted to each, and indeed their inclusion at all, is elusive and appears to be regulated by serendipity, rather than by planning.

> **66 Polish news bulletins are read at breakneck speed as if newscasters were being paid by the word. 99**

Polish weather is one of the few relatively stable elements in the nation, and weather forecasts suggesting that it would be worth taking an umbrella are usually right. They, too, are in the mass viewing bracket.

> **66 Scandals, particularly political ones, eat into air-time and are savoured with great gusto by viewers. 99**

Parliamentary proceedings are televised, with the predictable effect that the Polish powers-that-be are even less respected than before. Scandals, particularly political ones, eat into air-time: interminable parliamentary investigations are transmitted live and whole and are savoured with great gusto by viewers. No-one makes such a meal of scandals as the Poles.

A cheap way of filling broadcasting hours is the street interview. The Poles, delighted to be asked for their views, gladly step forward. There are opinion polls on virtually every aspect of Polish life: market research has come to town in a big way, but though the format delights, no-one has quite figured out what the object is or, indeed, that an object is needed.

Children's programmes, on the whole, are good. Presenters talk in normal voices, and guests are not dunked in green slime. A long-standing tradition is the 'goodnight story' at 7.30 p.m., the signal for the nation's parents to try to pack youngsters off to bed.

> **66 There are opinion polls on virtually every aspect of Polish life, but though the format delights, no-one has quite figured out what the object is or, indeed, that an object is needed. 99**

Unlike Western ones, padded with celebrities plugging something, Polish chat shows, in the land where the specialist is king, are full of specialists, talking about the subject they specialise in. But game shows are as vapid as elsewhere and reality TV as pervasive.

The Church, previously excluded, fills all residual televisual space; Mass and other religious ceremonies are not just reserved for Sunday viewing.

Homegrown soaps are popular and are in the British or Australian tradition – everyday lives of common folk – though they tend to feature the middle more than the working classes. To satisfy the persisting requirement for sagas about the exciting lives of unbelievably rich folk, Poles import South American soaps. These go out at an earlier time and are aimed at the women who are cooking dinner, to take them away, at least in thought, from the kitchen sink.

Going out

The Poles are avid theatre-goers, and the fare on offer is generally reasonable. Not all of it is sombre avant-garde although fringe theatre often takes the physical form of the tonal surrealism of the composer Penderecki.

66 To satisfy the persisting requirement for sagas about the exciting lives of unbelievably rich folk, Poles import South American soaps. 99

The Łódź Film School attracted students from all over the world and churned out so many of them that the credits of virtually any film made anywhere in the world list at least one Polish name.

People also love going to the opera and concerts and prefer to go in evening dress; they sit up straight and say 'Shhh' at the faintest crackling of sweet papers should anyone be so shameless as to take sweets in with them. Poles sit up straight and say 'Shhh' even at informal open-air concerts.

Communing with nature

In a country which has one third of its land covered in forests, no Pole is more than a bus ride away from one. Love of the forests lies deep in every Polish heart. They are a source of food, recreation, exports, and, if the worst comes to the worst, a bolt hole if an invader becomes too obnoxious.

The Polish countryside has a characteristic patchwork quilt appearance. Poland was the only country of the Eastern bloc that avoided land collectivisation and as there is no *jus primo geniture*, property is willed to all offspring equally. Thus sizeable estates could degenerate after a few generations into tiny strips consisting of two rows of beans, three of potatoes, etc., with two porkers and a cow tethered in the middle, all on less land than the average European farmer sets aside.

> **In a country which has one third of its land covered in forests, no Pole is more than a bus ride away from one.**

This process is now in reverse. As rural unemployment has emptied villages, the remaining farmers have expanded and automated and the patches on the quilt are growing in size and changing the landscape. The horse and cart have almost disappeared along with the back-bending hand-picking of crops, and the tractor and combine harvester are now the norm. Fortunately, the old fertilising ways have not yet died nor agri-business taken hold, so it has been relatively easy to revert to healthy organic farming.

Poland is one of the few countries in Europe that still has a self-proclaimed peasant class. Indeed, there is a peasant nestling in the heart of even the most noble Pole.

> **❝ There is a peasant nestling in the heart of even the most noble Pole. ❞**

Just as all sensible Poles ensure that they have a member of their kith and kin in every country they wish to visit, so they also kit themselves out with several near and dear ones tilling the land somewhere in Poland not too far away. This ensures that urban dwellers have fresh organic produce and the young have some grass to run around on.

Those lacking the foresight to have families in the country take advantage of the flourishing agro-tourism industry (invented to combat rural poverty) or invest in *działki* (allotments). The latter are beautifully tended, with a staggering array of crops, and the allotment shed, far from being a hotchpotch of rusty corrugated iron, is a palatial miniature house. The effect from a distance is of enchanting garden estates for pixies.

> **❝ From a distance, allotments resemble enchanting garden estates for pixies. ❞**

Urban Poles who live in tower blocks spend weekends, summer holidays and even their retirement at their allotments. Those who cannot afford even an allotment will turn the family graves into burgeoning riots of carefully tended floral tribute.

Sports

The most popular leisure activities are mountaineering, hill walking, sailing and skiing – all of which the sporty can indulge in without leaving the country.

Skiing was the competitive sport that especially seized the attention of viewers' because of Adam Małysz, world-class ski jumper, tiny by name (Małysz means 'little 'un') and by nature (5'5"), and cute with it. His success won the nation's heart and spawned a raft of new talent keen to imitate him.

> **The most popular leisure activities are hill walking, mountaineering, sailing and skiing – all of which the sporty can indulge in without leaving the country.**

Given their fondness for winter sports, it is surprising that there are not more such success stories. One justifiable reason the Poles hark back to Communism with nostalgia is sports provision. The scholarships and training facilities that were available to all talented youngsters have melted away in the heat of capitalism. Private sponsorship is still too rare.

> **The Poles are too anarchic to be keen team-game players.**

The Poles are too anarchic to be keen team-game players. If they must play team games, they choose volleyball or basketball. But they love football: once they have found 22 volunteers (or better still, 11 to pit against 11 from another nation), the populace can sit back in its armchair and indulge in epic bouts of criticism. This is why bridge is a national passion. It gives scope for the players to argue with partners and opponents alike.

Eating & Drinking

Food is thought to be a failure unless plentiful – nouvelle cuisine would never get past a Pole.

Polish food was designed to be filling. It took account of the cold, hard winters and sheer physical energy expended in daily living. The climate is still the same, but office life is decidedly less calorie-intensive than tilling the soil and gathering the harvest. Most traditional Polish cooking was heavy on preparation time as well as on the stomach, but doctors are now busy explaining how heavy it is on the heart, too, and meals are finally shrinking.

> **66 Food is thought to be a failure unless plentiful – nouvelle cuisine would never get past a Pole. 99**

Breakfast, taken at an ungodly hour because work starts early, is a selection of cold cuts of meat with bread and coffee. 'Second breakfast' is whatever you can get away with at work: usually another coffee and a sandwich at your desk, and if your desk happens to be in the front office of a bank, you eat in full public view.

Work finishes around 3 o'clock, and the main meal

of the day, *obiad* (dinner), is eaten as soon after as transport home allows. Soups as a first course are obligatory and substantial, and look as if they should be tackled with knife and fork. The most famous is *barszcz*, or beetroot. *Rosół* (chicken soup), as in the Jewish tradition, is said to be more than a soup: it is the medical and psychological equivalent of the English cup of tea.

For the second course, 'meat and two veg' is the norm – pork, beef, chicken, but not lamb. The Poles equate sheep with mutton, which they

> **66 Soups as a first course are obligatory and substantial, and look as if they should be tackled with knife and fork. 99**

declare (not unreasonably) smells. The alternative main course is pasta: dishes like *pierogi*, triangular sweet or savoury ravioli, known throughout Eastern Europe and universally, though wrongly, translated as dumplings.

Kolacja (cold-cuts), the last meal of the day, eaten any time between 6 p.m. and midnight, depends on the sleeping (or otherwise) habits of the family. Like breakfast, it consists mainly of bread, cheese, and cold meats. This is not as monotonous as it sounds for Poles have a bewildering variety of cold meats. They will smoke anything, and have as many varieties of sausage and hams as the French have cheeses.

The Poles love cheeses too and produce many and smoke some. The unique native cheese, *oscypek*, doubles as folk art – diamond shaped with folksy patterns embossed on it. It comes in two forms – soft and fresh, like dehydrated curd cheese with a salty tang, or hard and gratable, not unlike parmesan. They also market a bewildering range of creams, especially soured: for soups, for deserts, for sauces. Think of a culinary need and Poland produces a cream to fit.

Of traditional dishes *bigos* is usually rendered on menus as hunters' stew. Historically, *bigos* was made in a cauldron over a camp fire in the middle of a forest in winter. Hunters would arrive with a pot of sauerkraut and, adding to it whatever they had managed to bag, simmer it for several days, interrupting the process with spells of cooling it in the snow. Today, a low hotplate replaces the camp fire and the fridge makes do for the snowy wastes, but two days' cooking is still the recommended minimum. This is a good way of waking up jaded appetites on the third day of Christmas, and one of the best disguises for turkey left-overs.

66 Think of a culinary need and Poland produces a cream to fit. 99

The Poles pickle things – a throw-back to long, hard winters before refrigerators – gherkins, beetroot, cabbage, onions, mushrooms, anything. Most housewives have an atavistic urge to pickle something come the autumn. And if they don't pickle it, they preserve it in alcohol. Traditional Polish herbs are parsley, marjoram, bay leaves and masses of dill. Polish pickles are exported all over the globe and now everyone has learned that pickled cucumbers taste better with a sprig of dill in the bottle. Supermarkets offer a dazzling variety of imported seasonings and there is every sign that the next generation of Poles will grow up believing, along with other young Europeans, that curry is their traditional national dish. However, the Polish fight-back campaign is in place, with a marketing strategy so effective that Polish food is now available all over the world. *Kabanos* (pencil thin sausage) or *bigos* could be set to become the new curry.

Polish snails are not eaten, but collected and then packed off to France for the French to eat, a superior way of throwing them over the garden fence.

> **Most housewives have an atavistic urge to pickle something come the autumn. And if they don't pickle it, they preserve it in alcohol.**

Compôtes and cakes feature heavily, especially a sort of Swiss roll filled not with jam, but with ground poppy seeds mixed with dried fruit (figs, dates, raisins) and honey.

Fish, when it appears, is either pickled (herrings) or freshwater: carp, pike, salmon, trout. Though the Polish fishing fleet is one of the largest in the world, Poles have never quite taken to the fruits of the sea. When the government tried a poster campaign to overcome this, their slogan 'Eat cod' acquired the graffiti: 'Shit tastes even worse'.

The fruits of the forests, however, are held in high esteem. Berries and mushrooms of all sorts are collected avidly, and the most urbane of townspeople will know their nuts. If you get marooned on a desert island, choose a Pole as your companion and you will never go hungry.

Drinking and toasts

Breakfast coffee in many countries is a weak and milky affair. Not so in Poland where it consists of a generous spoonful of ground coffee heaped into a glass of boiling water. If your spoon does not stand up on its own, it is a failure. Experience teaches you when to stop sipping, just before you swallow the grounds.

> **66 Even the most urbane of townspeople will know their nuts. 99**

Tea is also taken without milk, served with lemon in a glass specially designed to ensure that you burn your fingers. Tea with milk is known as 'Bavarian' and considered only fit for breast-feeding mothers.

Vodka used to be consumed at home, which was only fair since much of it was brewed there. A child's chemistry set, described on the box as 'The Little Chemist', is still known as 'The Little Brewer'. However, the bars and pubs springing up in even the smallest towns are tempting many to wine and dine al fresco and in public.

Vodka is divided into two types: dry and clear for the men, theoretically at least (and this includes Bison vodka with the blade of grass in it), and sweet for the ladies. Beware Polish liquors. They are usually 40+% and drunk undiluted: firewater. Women might be seen to be sweeter toothed, but their heads have to be just as strong as the men's.

Technicoloured sweet vodkas can be made of virtually anything: ripe morello cherries, honey, nuts, lemon, hot chilli peppers. There is even one with bits of gold floating

66 Polish pure spirit, 90%, 189° proof, is the strongest drink known to man. Avoid drinking this neat without prior instruction and a soft landing. 99

in it. Those Poles who do buy their vodka in a shop often doctor it at home and create delicious home-made liquors. These are generally made with a base of Polish pure spirit, 90%, 180° proof, the nearest thing to pure alcohol possible, and the strongest drink known to man. Avoid drinking this neat without prior instruction and a soft landing.

The methodology of drinking is in tiny cut-crystal glasses, drained in one gulp, after a toast, and usually, sensibly, accompanied by lots of food. The Pole who sent his host's treasured Waterford flying into the grate is apocryphal. Poles hang on to their glasses to ensure refills. Rounds of toasts usually start with the health of the hosts, followed by the health of the guests, followed by the health of the beautiful ladies,

and the handsome gentlemen, then bachelor days.
After that, tradition leaves each dinner party to its own
devices.

Sense of Humour

The tone of most Polish humour is wry, dry and
frequently black – a form of whistling in the dark in
bleak situations. Poles see public figures, particularly
those in the political arena, as legitimate targets; after
all, no-one made run for office. Political satire, or the
great Polish Political Joke, which
under Communism was a substitute
for political debate, is emerging from
the state of hibernation it resorted to
when independence came. However,
current targets are social mores and lifestyle, both in
the process of monumental change. Hence corruption,
still rife in the medical profession, is the butt of this
joke:

> **66 Poles tell jokes
> against themselves –
> thus beating
> others to it. 99**

> Doctor: 'Yours is a very rare case that will enrich
>   medical science.'
>
> Patient: 'Will 200 *zloty* be enough, doctor?'

Poles tell jokes against themselves – thus beating
others to it. For example: the manager of a travelling
theatre complained that when he put on tragedies the
takings were comic, and when he tried showing come-

dies, they were tragic. As for subject matter, curiously, for all the awfulness of Polish plumbing, scatology features less in Poland than it does in France or Italy. But sex does, as do mothers-in-law:

'So what does your son-in-law do?'

'Exactly what I tell him.'

Fashions in humour come and go, but little Jasiu, scourge of the nursery, is ever precociously young. He even has his own web site.

Jasiu: 'Can five-year-old Basia be pregnant?'

Gynaecologist: 'Of course not.'

Jasiu: 'The rotten little blackmailer.'

Religion, too, features, and with an irreverent twist:

Confessor to young man: 'So how do you sin?'

Young man to confessor: 'Father, I came here to confess, not to boast.'

Priest: 'Children, what must we do before the priest can absolve us of our sins?'

Little Jasiu: 'Commit them, Father?'

Puns and word-play are hugely enjoyed, e.g: 'I read one of your poems.''The last one?' 'I hope so.'

Poland is one of the few places outside Britain where whimsy and nonsense are popular. Hence the cartoon of a wingless bird flying through the air and thinking: 'Why do I need a fridge when I haven't even got a phone?'

In the battle of the sexes, both are in flux, on a complementary roll of self-doubt and rudderlessness. As usual in Poland, doubts are turned into jokes:

After a major row with her spouse, a wife is soaking away her ire in a soothing bath. Emerging from the foam she looks in the long mirror: front, side, back, deep sigh, other side and then front again. Another deep sigh, followed by an explosive: 'Well, serve him bloody well right!'

As one might expect, jokes involving drinking and intoxication are legion:

'Excuse me, what time is it?'
'D'you know, I could do with a drink too.'

'Life begins at 50.' (50 grams is the standard measure of alcohol.)
'It's even better at a 100.'

Wife: 'You promised you'd change into a different man.'
Husband: 'I did. He drinks too.'

Diary of a visitor:
Monday: I went drinking with some Poles.
Tuesday: Hangover so bad, I almost died.
Wednesday: I went drinking with the Poles.
Thursday: If only I'd died on Tuesday.

What is Sold Where

These days Poles wheel trolleys round Western-style supermarkets and buy what they want when they can afford it, and there is no need to tote spare carrier bags and large amounts of cash at all times, just in case. A whole generation of children has never witnessed empty shelves and meat queues and their parents are happy for them. But when the kids are in bed and it's nostalgia time, many still have the odd pang of longing for the days when life was young and happiness was a kilo of ham, twelve rolls of lavatory paper or a bra which actually fitted, and everyone in the queue – the great leveller – was equal.

The times when virtually all goods in shops had instructions in every known language but Polish are also gone, and with

> **❝ These days there is no need to tote spare carrier bags and large amounts of cash at all times, just in case. ❞**

them the guesswork: 'Is it a tube of mayonnaise or hæmorrhoid cream?' Some quaint anomalies remain to amuse the intrepid shopper, such as signs announcing that the shop sells leather goods when from the contents it is clearly a florist. The disappearance of some shops or, indeed, whole buildings may be the 'mafia', or more correctly, the mafias, who have been known to assist the unco-operative to early retirement. As one satirist explained: 'Before, there was one mafia, and everyone knew who, where and why: it was the Central Committee of the Communist Party. Now there's the Wołomin mafia, the Pruszków mafia, visiting mafias from over the border…'

Health & Hygiene

Most Poles are amazingly well-informed hypochondriacs. Not only will they tell you in great detail exactly what is wrong with them and how their ailments are being treated, if you don't stop them in time they will also tell you exactly what you should be doing about all yours.

Poles tend to specialise in one complaint, and not only will they know more about it than many a Western professor, they will be best friends with, or related to, the most eminent specialist in the country, who they will quote extensively.

" Most Poles are amazingly well-informed hypochondriacs. "

Polish doctors do not seem to mind being accosted with medical queries at parties or in public places, and will happily agree that your manifestation of the disease is the most interesting they have ever come across. The ultimate example of this was the doctor passing through a cemetery who was hailed by a voice from a grave asking for a cure for worms.

The Poles' knowledge of treatments will encompass the oldest herbal remedies and the latest Western drugs. It is worth listening – they are usually right. Polyclinics, equipped with the latest technology, flexible appointment systems and, as private health care goes, comparatively modest fees, have sprouted all over Poland, and Poles frequent them as regularly and as often as they go to church. They feel compelled to keep their finger on the pulse, and while they're at it, check up on their blood pressure, cholesterol, insulin levels, kidney efficiency – anything and everything that can, and therefore should, be measured.

> **Poles feel compelled to keep their finger on the pulse, and while they're at it, check up on their blood pressure, cholesterol, insulin levels, kidney efficiency...**

The place to get hold of the potion you have been recommended is a pharmacy. While a number of hospitals are still rather grubby, sad places, most drug stores have floors you would not mind eating off and where the light bounces off every gleaming bottle and ampoule. On sale are the products of the world's leading laboratories alongside every alternative medicine known to man. If a queue is to be found anywhere in Poland, it will be here, as the pharmacist advises customers at length and expertly on anything that might be ailing them. Queuers seldom complain – they are too busy eavesdropping.

For those too busy to haunt their local pharmacy, health products dominate television. Over half of all advertising time is taken up with them, with those purporting to cure short- and long-term effects of alcohol leading the fray, followed by palliatives for the ravages of old age, such as herbs to cure fading eyesight and, of course, rejuvenating creams. Much of the other half of viewing time is taken up with financial contrivances such as insurance to pay for all these nostrums.

If you have to go into hospital, make arrangements for your meals to be sent in, or else prepare to go on an unscheduled diet. Be prepared too, to bribe the doctor, nurse and cleaning lady or you could find yourself in a corridor with a dust sheet over you. Tackling bribery in the health service has proved to be one of the most obdurate targets for reform, despite draconian government measures, including arresting and handcuffing a leading cardiologist mid-heart transplant.

> **❝ If you go into hospital, make arrangements for your meals to be sent in, or else prepare to go on an unscheduled diet. ❞**

Best by far to stick to less lethal diseases and the private clinics which, having given you a print-out of the state of all your internal organs, should this be unfavourable, will provide the names and consulting times of the leading specialist in your chosen affliction.

Running water

Polish hand basins have no plugs because the Poles wash in running water. Basins and baths all have mixer taps so you are not scalded, and the hot water supply often runs off the local generating station so is ecologically and economically sound. It used to be free, and is still cheap.

Away from home the wise carry emergency lavatory paper with them. Public plumbing, though improved beyond compare, is still able to surprise. Public conveniences are staffed by formidable ladies who will, in exchange for a pre-ordained sum that is usually marked on a piece of cardboard somewhere near their person, hand over sheets of grey lavatory paper – splinters optional.

> **❝ There is no such thing as a Pole with normal blood pressure. ❞**

The atmosphere

The popular explanation for most woes in Poland is pressure. This does not mean stress, though if any people can justifiably claim to be stressed, the Poles can. This is the atmospheric variety. '*Ciśnienie*' is chanted mantra-like as the basis for any number of ills, from varicose veins to the state of the economy. High and low blood pressure sufferers alike claim to be ruled by the barometer, and there is no such thing as a Pole with normal blood pressure. High blood

pressure sufferers will quote, ad nauseam, the latest
health warnings about the damage their bodies are
undergoing, but they will never act upon them. Thus:
'I shouldn't really be eating this, but...' is the general
refrain. Sufferers from low blood pressure knock back
cups of coffee that would make a horse reel, without
apparent ill effect, explaining that it is the only way to
keep their circulation going.

Culture

Publish and be overwhelmed

Writing, be it in the form of newspaper, periodical or
book, is the vein through which Polish life-blood (i.e.,
words) flows. It is axiomatic that three Poles on a
desert island will form four political parties (of which
two will be coalitions and one a splinter group) and
each will have its own newspaper, journal and series
of occasional publications.

> **66 Writing is the vein through which Polish life-blood (i.e., words) flows. 99**

Behind every writer lurks a publisher, and behind every publisher
an archivist. Libraries mark the
presence, or even the mere passage,
of Poles throughout the world. The Standing
Conference of Museums, Libraries and Archives
Outside Poland has members all over the globe.

A Polish house is not a home without its bookcase,

and one shelf will be devoted to the classics, more often than not Henryk Sienkiewicz, the Polish Walter Scott. Known abroad by *Quo Vadis* rather than by name, he was translated into English and published by an American with the unlikely name of Jeremiah Curtin. One of the first international best-sellers on a modern scale, his works were (and still are) repeatedly filmed, but he earned little from them because of Poland's copyright laws, or rather, the lack of them. Beloved for his *Trylogia* set in the days of Poland's glory in the 17th century, many Poles can and do recite whole chunks of him.

Another *sine qua non* of every domestic bookcase is Adam Mickiewicz, a revolutionary Romantic, exiled with Chopin and others after the 1830 November Revolution, to Paris, where he penned wonderfully evocative descriptions of the Poland of his childhood:

'Fatherland, you are like health itself. Only he knows your true worth, who has lost you.'

His early works still have power and relevance: the 1968 Warsaw students' revolt opened at a performance of his play *Dziady*. Here are a few random stanzas of his epic poem *Pan Tadeusz*:

One happiness remains: when evening greys,
You sit with a few friends and lock the door,
And by the fireside shut out Europe's roar,
Escape in thought to happier time and tide,
And muse and dream of your own countryside.

49

A typical Polish anomaly is Joseph Conrad, writer of sublime English, who wanted to be seen as a Polish author fighting his country's corner. A more recent addition to the classic canon is Wisława Szymborska, 1996 Nobel laureate. She entitled one of her poems *Conversation with a stone*. Another simply states:

> The joy of writing
> The power of preserving
> Revenge of a mortal hand.

Music

For a nation with fairly modest, popular, musical ability, Poland is home to a decent array of world-class composers and musicians, from the ubiquitous Chopin, through Paderewski (inter-war president and proof positive that Poles are better off ruled by musicians than electricians) to the modernists Lutosławski and Penderecki – regarded as acquired tastes – or the modern but more traditional Górecki.

Polish pop music, though a feeble mirror of Western fashion with occasional flashes of originality, is experimenting with a fusion of folk, especially Góral music, and reggae, which seems to work surprisingly well.

Poland never gave up on jazz and Polish musicians are now leading the international jazz revival – which may be why Nigel Kennedy has made his home there.

Film-making

Under Communism, making films in Poland was a risky business. Censorship was fierce, so Polish directors resorted to powerful symbolism and elaborate allegory. Today, censorship has long gone but mastery of visual symbolism is still a key skill of the Polish film-makers' craft. The daddy of them all, Andrzej Wajda, relayed to the world the bleak reality of Polish life, in particular his *Man of Marble* (1977), life under Stalin, and *Man of Steel* (1981) set

> **Censorship has long gone but mastery of visual symbolism is still a key skill.**

during marshal law. For light relief, he directed gems from Polish literature like *The Wedding* and *Pan Tadeusz* which depict earlier, happier times. He set the tone and standard for those who followed in his footsteps into the international arena, amongst others: Polanski, Zanussi, Skolimowski and Kieślowski, many of whom also veered between a gloomy reality and a glorified past.

Multi-award winner Agnieszka Holland initially ploughed her own furrow. After graduating, however, she joined the rest – a cliquey bunch, who acted in each other's movies, wrote each other's scripts and adopted each other's imagery, many of them contributors to the 'Cinema of Moral Anxiety' (c.1974-81), whose name could aptly be used to summarise the totality of the oeuvres of Polish film-makers.

Architecture

The Poles not only defend their historical city centres from the passage of time and progress, they lovingly rebuild the depredations of other less sentimental nations. After the Second World War they recreated Warsaw and Gdańsk. However, though there are medieval towns with façades as yet unspoilt by McDonald's yellow arches, much of Poland is now lit up with neon.

Neo-brutalist Soviet architecture was an even greater disaster than the aberrations reigning at the time in the West, and its heritage of serried ranks of heavy, concrete blocks of flats still march across the land-scape. Attempts to jolly up their façades are testing Polish ingenuity, but with some measure of success. Old houses were knocked down or left to rot, so the only alternative was self-build. Town planners allowed for few models, all with the same boxy, flat-roofed silhouette that every owner now feels duty bound to modify – their roof-lines swoop like roller-coasters as neighbour outdoes neighbour.

66 New homes range from faux Le Corbusier to Dallas-style haciendas – and everyone is at it. 99

New homes range from the tasteful to the ridiculous, faux Le Corbusier to Dallas-style haciendas – and everyone is at it. Even mouldering ruins are being bought and refurbished. It seems as if the whole country is a vast building site.

National Heroes

It is ironic that many of Poland's most famous sons
and daughters went by non-Polish-sounding names
and are therefore not immediately associated with the
country at all. France is the fiercest counter-claimant:
Chopin had a French father and surname, but his
upbringing, heart and prominent nose were Polish. In
Poland he is known as Szopen.

Marie Curie-Skłodowska, dis-
coverer of radium, was all
Polish. The non-Polish element
of her name came from her
husband, Pierre Curie, and the

> **66 Chopin had a French
> father and surname, but
> his upbringing, heart
> and prominent nose
> were Polish. 99**

Poles are fighting a rear-guard action with the Marie
Curie Foundation to get them to incorporate the name
she was born under. Copernicus (Kopernik in Polish)
was a Pole from Polish Toruń. The Germans, who
claim the town was from time to time German and
therefore so is Copernicus, are treated as vexatious
litigants and just plain silly. The Swedes, during their
excursion into Polish lands, looted Kopernik's library,
which is now in Uppsala. Their excuse for hanging on
to it – that Poland is unsafe because everyone keeps on
looting it – makes a warped kind of sense.

More people associate Kosciuszko with a mountain
in Australia than with a Pole who fought for Polish
and American independence. Few non-Poles know

that King Canute was half Polish as was Bonnie Prince Charlie (both on their mother's side). Conrad wrote in English and anglicised his name, and who can blame him? Would he have been as widely read if he'd been published under Korzeniowski?

Tit for tat, Poles make sure that any foreigner entering a Polish library catalogue becomes a naturalised Pole, so Shakespeare becomes Szekspir, while Winnie the Pooh turns into Kubuś Puchatek.

In Poland itself the only way to ensure continued popularity is to be dead. Then your portrait will be hung everywhere and streets will be named after you.

> **In Poland the only way to ensure continued popularity is to be dead.**

The heroes Communism forced upon the nation have been expunged from signposts, maps and pedestals, and the old heroes reinstated, but there has been no revenge-taking even on the most hated of the old guard.

The joke about General Jaruzelski asking his portrait what would become of them both, and receiving the answer, 'They'll take me down and hang you instead', has not come true. Poles are not vengeful by nature; nor do they seek out feet of clay in their chosen heroes, but forgive them their (minor) trespasses.

What they cannot forgive is heroes who let the side down abroad. Lech Wałęsa was given a long rope. The Poles were always aware of his limitations and just crossed their fingers and hoped that he would manage to get by in foreign palaces, but when he turned pompous and pretentious with it, he became the butt of a legion of jokes. The Duck twins, president and prime minister, embarrassed themselves and the nation both at home and abroad but it was their transgressions abroad that are not forgiven.

Leszek Balcerowicz, architect of the Polish economic miracle in the eyes of the international banking world, is another matter. A brilliant economist, he is liked as a person but loathed as a financial reformer – despite the fact that his reforms spectacularly paid off.

> **Even atheists, agnostics and various species of 'don't knows' believed in '*their*' Pope.**

Popes, especially Polish popes, are the exception that proves the rule. Even atheists, agnostics and various species of 'don't knows' believed in '*their*' Pope. Where Wałęsa was Poland's maverick son who could not be trusted to remember which knife to use and when, Wojtyła was the clever one who could always be relied on to talk intelligently and hold his own, even amongst foreigners, however posh they might be. As for holding somewhat idiosyncratic views on sex, well, even heroes are allowed the odd foible or two.

Witnessed by every Pole in the universe, the Papal funeral was the last chance for the nation to reflect on the glory of the man, and the first shot in the campaign for his canonisation.

Conversation & Gestures

On average, the Poles gesticulate a bit more than the French and a bit less than the Spanish.

A number of signs convey that you are just about to seek alcoholic sustenance (such as pinging your throat with a flick of your thumb and forefinger), or that the other fellow has already done so, far too liberally. If your shaggy dog story is met by a palm held waist-high, first face-down, then face-up, your audience is telling you that when they were 'so' high, the joke had a beard 'that' long.

66 The enigmatic English: 'Don't teach your Grandma how to suck eggs', is rendered more graphically in Polish as: 'Don't teach your father how to make children.' 99

Some sayings translate exactly from Polish into English. 'Small beer' is *'małe piwo'* which means 'small beer' – though why this should be so it is hard to say. 'Wolf' is cried in the same way, and 'dear' has the same double meaning of 'beloved' and 'expensive'. However, some sayings are improved in the Polish version; for instance, the enigmatic English: 'Don't teach your Grandma how to suck eggs', is rendered more graphically in Polish as: 'Don't teach your father how to make children.'

The words *'Na zdrowie'*, literally 'To your health', are said for 'Cheers', but also as 'Bless you' when someone sneezes. Small boys with runny noses who haven't got a hanky say out loud: 'King Sobieski had a moustache' (sleeve rubbed under the nose), 'and a long sword' (sleeve rubbed downwards along the trousers).

Most anatomical references are directly translatable. The commonest 'soft' swear-word (the equivalent of 'shit') is *'cholera'* –

> **66 The commonest 'soft' swear-word (the equivalent of 'shit') is *'cholera'*. 99**

presumably from the time it was endemic, which fortunately it no longer is. *'Ale jaja'*, literally 'What bollocks', is said more in admiration than condemnation, for example in response to a good tall story.

There are some people in Poland who can swear entertainingly for an hour without repeating themselves, but this ability seems to be linked more to professions than to nationality: troopers, plumbers and doctors leading the fray.

The questioning of the victim's paternity, the virtue of his or her mother, and graphic descriptions of what can be placed where, are the most popular themes. The fad for using the word *'kurwa'* (whore) as a punctuation mark is an egalitarian trend used by doctor and dustman alike, and mainly, though not exclusively, by males. So overused is it that it has lost its meaning and it is said that one teller of an anecdote, having said *'kurwa'* every third word throughout, was stuck for a description when he actually wanted to say 'whore', and resorted to 'lady of the night'.

Custom & Tradition

Religion

An old truism claims that Poles believe not in God, but the Madonna. Certainly the cult of the Madonna is strong: there are many more pictures and statues of her than of the rest of the Holy Family, and in 1717 she was even officially crowned Queen of Poland.

The nation has a pragmatic attitude to religion. There is a church or place of worship somewhere in Poland for virtually every denomination, and a range of sects – from Moonies to evangelists of every hue – is gaining ground amongst the young.

> **In good times Poles treat God much like roué nephews treat spinster aunts – with the odd respectful nod and bouquet as a hedge against future expectations.**

The Poles, like many others, are decidedly more religious in times of need. They perform the rituals assiduously but only go along with those parts of the dogma that suit them. Hence contraception was never a problem: swallow the Pill, proceed in the usual manner, and then confess all. In good times they treat God much like roué nephews treat spinster aunts – with the odd respectful nod and bouquet as a hedge against future expectations.

When the Communists rather foolishly tried to stop the Poles from practising their religion, the churches filled to overflowing. 'Forbidden' is a term of encouragement to a Pole. Now that this kind of protest is no longer necessary, churches are slowly emptying and, despite the 'Wojtyła factor', will soon be left to old ladies and tourists, just like the rest of Europe, though the Church is fighting its corner hard.

> **66 'Forbidden' is a term of encouragement to a Pole. 99**

The increasingly vocal interest (some would call it meddling) of the Church in politics – a battle between Church and State for hearts, minds and power – is turning previously pious folk against the clergy. Perceived clerical greed (priests are battling for state salaries) doesn't help. Nor does the fact that the church authorities haven't or can't do anything about Poland's troublesome priest, Father Rydzyk, whose reactionary Radio Marija and TV station have also alienated many. The anti-abortion legislation, forced through the *Sejm* (Parliament) against considerable opposition, earned the Church the sort of opprobrium previously reserved for the Communist Party.

Despite this, much of Polish social life still revolves round the parish church, for where else can you show off your latest outfit or car, meet your friends for a gossip, or flirt? Most festivals and public life hang on its calendar. It's the pageantry, pomp and circumstance of Roman Catholicism that appeal most to the Poles. Protestantism never stood a chance – much too grey.

Holy days

Poles still follow the ancient European way of celebrating the winter festival now known as Christmas. The opening shot of festivities comes on Christmas Eve – no meat, but rather too much of everything else. After this, the winter festival is in full swing, with all office, institutional and any other parties being held after Christmas, which cheers up bleak January and February. Decorations are not taken down till Our Lady of the Candles (Candlemas) on 2nd February, when candles are lit in windows to keep away the wolves. Everything comes to a glorious close on Fat Thursday before Lent, with carnival and doughnuts.

> **❝ 'Robć szopkę'
> (to make a crib), is
> Polish slang for
> making a fuss. ❞**

At Christmas each Polish church has a crib *(szopka)* and strives and connives to have the best in the neighbourhood. Families trail from church to church to admire and (of course) criticise them. The parish priest of a Wrocław church, an avid collector of clockwork toys, takes over an entire side chapel and his crib marches, nods, bongs and bows in perpetual motion. Kraków cribs are elaborate confections with tiny silver foil figures housed in edifices that echo Kraków's spires and onion domes. They are judged at annual competitions and the best end up as museum pieces. *'Robić szopkę'* (literally 'to make a crib'), which elsewhere might conjure up images of a humble stable with shepherds and sheep, is Polish slang for making a fuss.

Christmas would not be Christmas without the Midnight Mass, when citizens weave their way to church after Wigilia, a traditional 12-course feast. Miracles occur annually: no church has yet spontaneously combusted, despite the air being 90° proof.

All Poles know all the words to the Christmas carols, but sadly, unlike the Welsh, Italians and Russians, they are not noted for their choral abilities. However, enthusiasm and volume make up for the lack of vocal talent.

Easter in Poland is still a religious festival and worship takes place in church rather than the DIY megastore. Folk

66 On Easter Monday Poles pour water over each other. You can come home drenched. 99

wandering around with baskets containing three-course meals are either going to feed their relatives in hospital or, if it's Easter Saturday, going to church to have their Sunday breakfast blessed. On Easter Monday Poles (mostly the young ones) pour water over each other. It's a custom that reaches back to pagan times, and you can come home drenched.

Corpus Christi is an excuse for little girls to air their Communion dresses, before they grow out of them, by parading through the town. Numerous parishes and many occupations have their own patron saint who is celebrated with colourful processions, for example, firemen celebrate St. Florian on 4th May and Silesians hold parades on 4th December, St. Barbara's Day, as she is the patron saint of miners.

Each parish, village and town also has its little wayside shrine, decked out with fresh flowers, even in remote mountain passes and woodlands, often with a plaque to mark atrocities of the distant past or recent car crashes.

> **66 Death is, logically enough, the second most popular topic of conversation after health. 99**

The top Polish saint is Our Lady. Top shrine is an icon, the Black Madonna of Częstochowa, a Polish Lourdes, which attracts pilgrims from all over the country, many on foot. When in 1981 the wearing of *Solidarność* badges was forbidden by martial law, the people wore badges of Our Lady of Częstochowa instead. Or electronic resistors – the name said it all – and Lech Wałęsa was an electrician, after all.

Deaths

Deaths are announced in newspapers, on black-edged posters pinned to walls and trees in town centres and on the front gate. These can either give the time and place of the funeral or they can be 'In memoriam'. Funerals are widely attended and death is, logically enough, the second most popular topic of conversation after health. Insurance companies have yet to discover how much the elderly fear a pauper's grave, so funeral parlours sell burial plots, complete with (as yet un-inscribed) memorial stones. A few of the ultra-lonely have been known to tend to their own graves and light candles on them.

On the gate to the cemetery in Zakopane is the motto: 'A nation is a people and its graves'. Poles revere their ancestors and 1st November, All Souls' Day (a.k.a. National Traffic Jam Day), is celebrated all over Poland. Families trek from one end of the country to the other, and even come from other countries, to visit family graves, and they spend hours planning elaborate itineraries to fit everyone in. The glow from the candles in larger cemeteries can be seen for miles.

> **Poles revere their ancestors. On All Souls' Day the glow from the candles in larger cemeteries can be seen for miles.**

Cemeteries are almost never empty. Families tend graves as carefully as they do their front gardens and the tombs of well-loved national figures, especially children's authors, are regularly visited and decked with school badges, flowers and candles. Some tomb-stones are real works of art. Sometimes schools and scout groups are given a cemetery to look after, in particular the graves of families who have died out or moved away.

Some cemeteries, such as Powązki in Warsaw, where the dead of the Warsaw Uprising lie, are national monuments. The simple crosses, with inscriptions such as 'Soldier, aged 14', are unbearably moving.

Holidays

The Poles have a fair selection of civic festivals, many in honour of battles, won or lost. Voted top by 60% of the nation is Constitution Day, 3rd May. The Communists tried to supplant this with International Labour Day on 1st May (known in Poland as the Workers' April Fool's Day), when school children and workers were driven into the streets and told to march and wave flags. This bit so deeply into the Polish psyche that it was commonly felt to be the most universal manifestation of oppression. There are recorded cases of dissidents encasing limbs in plaster to avoid attending. But it goes against the Polish grain to discard any holiday from the pack, whatever its origin, so by way of compromise many Poles now celebrate all three days – from the 1st to the 3rd.

> **❝ Totally unknown until a few decades ago St. Valentine's Day took off like a rocket. ❞**

With their usual enthusiasm for finding new ways of celebrating anything, Poles have taken to commercial festivals in a big way. Totally unknown until a few decades ago, Valentine's Day took off like a rocket – all those cards and flowers – and is now so firmly established that even the Post Office joins in by issuing special stamps with hearts and roses.

Children's Day is marked by a day off school. Most schools arrange a programme of visits and outings, and the children are allowed a certain amount of behavioural leeway. They do not as yet receive presents on Children's Day. What with birthdays, name-days, St. Nicholas (6th December, when presents appear under pillows), Christmas, Holy Communion and Confirmation, Polish children do well enough already. Parents thank heaven that they don't know about the tooth fairy – yet.

> **The habit of name-days has advantages: if clever or greedy, you can manage two parties and sets of presents a year.**

Bearing gifts

Instead of birthdays, the Poles have the very civilised habit of celebrating name-days – which has several advantages:

- calendars note the saint of the day, which reminds you who you should ring or visit,
- no-one asks your age when it's your turn,
- if clever or greedy, you can manage two parties and sets of presents a year.

Poles do not hand greetings cards to people with their gifts. Cards are for sending to those you are not in physical contact with. Flowers are for handing to people. Flower shops are everywhere and flowers are bought for name-days, birthdays, anniversaries, greetings, partings, when popping in to see a friend, or just because you feel like it.

On International Women's Day, another former Communist festival, the usual procedure is for men to buy flowers for as many women as they can afford to: wife, mistress, mother, secretary, friends; and a bottle of vodka for themselves. The director of a large factory who wanted to please all his women workers allegedly read a prepared speech then gave a bouquet to each one of the 700 workers on the first shift, but in the middle of the second shift he had a heart attack and dropped dead, thus unintentionally giving the workers the best present of all – the rest of the day off.

> **❝ On International Women's Day, men buy flowers for as many women as they can afford to. ❞**

Assistants in florist shops the world over are bewildered by the number of men buying big bunches of roses on this day, even handing them out to women passing by. Only Poles know why.

Folk art

Peasant traditions, dances and art are cherished and kept going. Some people can still perform a Krakowiak or a spirited Mazurka and most have an impressive repertoire of folk songs. But gone are the days when every home came equipped with a regional folk costume for high and holy days. The network of state support for folk artists, like so much of the Communist infrastructure of subsidies for worthy causes, has collapsed. Yet there are still many towns and villages where, on various holy days, over-voluptuous ladies insist on parading through town in the wake of a Madonna or some other icon, as if they were still young maidens. Not all of them do this with an eye to the tourist trade.

> **66 On holy days some over-voluptuous ladies parade through town in the wake of a Madonna, as if they were still young maidens. 99**

Folk art is by no means dead. One way or another, all Polish homes have a little something that is folksy in origin: a *pasiak* (brightly striped folkweave throws from Łowicz), a tablecloth of primary coloured cabbage roses, a teapot or plate displaying customary patterns or even a bookmark decorated with paper cut-out cockerels. The item may be stylised almost beyond recognition, but it will be there, ready to be dragged out for Christmas, Easter, the Third of May or any other occasion, whether religious, patriotic or social, which needs a boost to make it more authentic or more fun.

Poles cling to tradition. Archaeologists examining the stomach contents of a prehistoric bog man found boiled wheat, poppy seeds, nuts and honey, in other words, *'kutia'*, still an essential Eastern Polish Christmas Eve dish.

Systems

Transport

Although the Poles travel extensively, they do not believe in travelling light. Only a Pole would try to convince airport check-in staff that a microwave constitutes hand luggage, in addition to a large holdall and five carrier bags. And only a Pole would succeed.

Nevertheless, cheap flight merchants have brought a new phenomenon – the Polish frequent traveller, who saunters through airports with a lightweight holdall and a smile, secure in the knowledge that a full set of necessities, from toothpaste to spare boots, awaits him at both ends of his journey. For heavy transporting of gifts, etc., Poles now resort to the surprisingly cheap and efficient parcel service.

> **Only a Pole would try to convince airport check-in staff that a microwave constitutes hand luggage. And only a Pole would succeed.**

The occasional tiny Fiat 126, once the most popular car in Poland, can still be spotted trundling around. With a roof rack laden to double its height and twice its length, it warms the heart. It once transported a nation.

The national rail service has undergone a transformation and trains are now clean and on time. They are also expensive and therefore fairly empty, so the authorities have 'discovered' marketing. Free coffee and a biscuit on the express probably costs little to lay on but makes an excellent impression.

Local transport is full to bursting. Trams course through most towns, alongside the ubiquitous bendy bus, the second half of which is best avoided even in Poland's more or less perpendicular streets, as the whiplash it generates is awesome.

> **66 The second half of the ubiquitous bendy bus is best avoided even in Poland's more or less perpendicular streets. 99**

The Warsaw metro, one of Europe's major long-playing transport dramas (alongside the Channel Tunnel) is now running a regular service and its users have forgotten the troubles involved. Talk of extending it to a network is seen as a sensible proposal – albeit a long-term one – and not a joke.

Green matters

The Poles are basically a rural nation, and the devastation and pollution caused by Communist industrialisation was deeply felt by the whole population. Much of this legacy has been eradicated, the most toxic industries in the more sensitive areas being the first to be shut down. The golden roof of Kraków's Wawel Castle is no longer pitted by acid fall-out from the foundries nearby, and even industrial Katowice is cleaner now that so many of its factories and mines lie dormant. However, the aftermath of the USSR's social engineering lives on: Silesia's unemployed have only pure air to console them.

The Poles had expected that Germany would help in the clean-up. It made sense that the country into which your pollution flowed would be first with assistance. The Germans, however, having their own unified pollution to deal with, were not in a position to aid the polluters further upstream until they had resolved the mess further down, illogical though that was in physical terms. And this was not the end of it: beyond Poland's borders still lie the even more polluted, radioactive lands of the Ukraine and Russia...

> **The Germans were not in a position to aid the polluters further upstream until they had resolved the mess further down.**

The children of the two worst affected areas are within just a few hours' drive of the fresh air of the Tatra Mountains. They are taken there for at least two weeks of the school year to give their lungs a fighting chance.

Recycling

Rediscovered now by the rest of the Western world, recycling never went out of fashion in Poland for purely economic reasons. As early as the 1970s, Coca-Cola plants were set up complete with attendant bottling and re-bottling plants and, despite the advent of cartons and plastic containers, the collection and return of glass bottles provides a source of revenue for the nation's children.

Polish men still tinker in sheds and make and mend things. The average Polish mechanic can and does construct something useful out of the equivalent of the contents of a Western scrap yard.

Education

An oft-quoted Jesuit saying states 'Give me a child at seven, and he is mine for life.' The Polish educational system, like most in Europe, was based on the Jesuit model. Today, however, the State wants to go one better so compulsory education starts at the age of six with the so-called 'zero' classes. The impetus behind this is as much economic as educational, i.e: the childcare needs of working parents.

Polish educational reform is in a constant state of flux, not to say free fall. The present state of play is that schools are divided into age bands, from six to thirteen, thirteen to sixteen, and sixteen to nineteen, leading to the *Matura,* the matriculation exam (similar to and as stressful as the French baccalauréat, both in style and wide range of subjects, and the devastating

> 66 The average Polish mechanic can and does construct something useful out of the equivalent of the contents of a Western scrap yard. 99

71

effect it has on the entire family of the sitter).

Tertiary education follows, a labyrinth of public and private initiative and enterprise which few students and even fewer parents can follow. Ostensibly the motivation of the government is the improvement of education standards but the fact that it also muddies the unemployment statistics and keeps them looking favourable is undoubtedly a welcome bonus.

> **Starting school comparatively late in life, Poles finish it even later, and sometimes never.**

Starting school comparatively late in life, Poles finish it even later, and sometimes never. Eternal students are numerous. The first university degree you can get is a *licencjat*, awarded after 3 years study, then a Master's after 5, and then a doctorate; after which come several echelons of even more rarefied doctorates or professorships. One can also specialise in each and every subject, and all such specialists publish papers – endlessly.

The educational system is beset with the problem common to every other area of Polish life – chronic underfunding. Abysmally paid, the teaching profession cannot attract or keep good staff. Having tried teaching in shifts and failed, bussing is now in vogue: closing small village schools and replacing them with larger, better equipped centralised schools.

The national curriculum, not so long ago cast in iron, is being smelted down all over the place. Wider ranges of subjects are being introduced alongside new technology though money considerations are slowing down the latter and aspirations have overtaken possibilities. Allegedly overheard in a school: 'From today children, we will learn mathematics with the help of computers. So, Jasiu, tell me, what is three computers added to six computers?'

In one brilliant display of their skills, Warsaw police shot three escaped tigers and a vet.

There is also a vast range of private classes in virtually anything – arts and crafts, aerobics, aromatherapy. The most prolific and popular are business, marketing and computers, whether at home or abroad. As employers no longer pay bonuses to those with degrees, many young people choose to attend such classes rather than go to university. Many do both. The whole of Poland seems to be studying something.

Crime & Punishment

The police force lacks the social kudos and salary structure to attract high flyers and is consequently low in numbers and brain cells. Yet the once inexhaustible well of police jokes has run dry, maybe because reality beats satire hollow: in one brilliant display of their skills, Warsaw police shot three escaped tigers and a vet.

Mainly because of its position on the crossroads between East and West, Poland features frequently and highly on international crime league tables. The nation can be found on the 'must see' list of drug dealers travelling East to West, especially those whose mind-altering substances of choice are amphetamines, whilst much of the luxury stolen car trade trundles West to East. Mercedes are firm favourites amongst the *mafioski* and Merc owners outside the fraternity are almost certain to be periodically relieved of them. Helpful police will direct victims to the man who will, at a price, retrieve the vehicle from the one who stole it. Owners of lesser cars are now pretty safe from depredation, though not so long ago Poles in full evening dress could be seen taking the more 'attractive' parts of their vehicles to concerts to ensure continued ownership of them.

> **❝ Poles in full evening dress could be seen taking the more 'attractive' parts of their vehicles to concerts to ensure continued ownership of them. ❞**

On the road

Latest statistics place Poland at the top of the 'My traffic jam is worse than your traffic jam' league in a survey that ranks world road congestion. By the end of a hot summer, the weight of the through-traffic bearing both legitimate and stolen goods and Western expertise from West to East, and raw materials and disillusioned bankers and entrepreneurs from East to West, is imprinted on Polish asphalt. Drivers know that they stray from the canyons worn in the tarmac at their peril – or that of their cars' suspension.

The new hazard of an excess of fledgling drivers has seen off the older one of the Polish peasant who viewed the highway, including motorways, as his own, and was apt to launch out with a horse-drawn cart as laden as Constable's *Haywain*, or with a herd of cows, with a careless disregard for life and limb.

A specific hazard on the roads used to be the road police who lurked behind bushes and leapt out in front of the unwary, lollipop held aloft, to exact instant fines (which some treated as pocket money). But now that gangs of no-gooders have taken to donning police uniforms and stopping passing motorists to hijack or rob them, the legitimate police force has been forced to advise motorists to ignore the lollipop.

> **The drivers know that they stray from the canyons worn in the tarmac at their peril – or that of their cars' suspension.**

Minor offences, such as jay walking, are also punished by on-the-spot fines. Drunk driving is increasing, despite the draconian penalties which start with heavy fines and end with imprisonment, and Polish prisons are no guest houses. Sentient Poles operate rotas at parties. Soft drinks are laid on for those who have drawn the short, sober straw. Even so, the statistics show that the number of cars and accidents are up a third, year on year. It's not the drunkenness that's the problem, it's the bad driving.

Business

After the economic disasters in Russia and the East, the much-vaunted Polish economic tiger has had to draw in its claws and unemployment figures are high, but the general mood is still buoyant. Young Poles believe that they can achieve anything, if they put their mind to it.

From a standing start in the early 1990s of having virtually no private industry at all, the Poles managed to open around two million private companies. Many went to the wall a day later. Most were one-man-and-his-dog affairs. Some can now be called 'big business'. The glass industry was one of the first to be turned around from a cripple into a thriving concern. Today, no self-respecting Western store is without pieces of Krosno glass, and lesser glass-making companies send their industrial spies to copy Krosno designs. IBM and Microsoft declared amnesties on copyright in order to stop Polish bootleg software, then established legitimate

> **From a standing start, Poles managed to open around two million private companies. Many went to the wall a day later.**

usage by offering generous discounts. Now many of the world's computer firms assemble and even produce in Poland.

In the shipbuilding industry, where it all began, the Szczecin Shipyard has held its own and is expanding. Bits of the Gdańsk Shipyard still function, but large chunks are being developed into loft apartments for young Polish professionals.

The world's companies still beat a path to Poland in search of cheaper labour. Meanwhile innumerable Poles seek work all over the world, and euros, pounds or dollars earned on

66 At Christmas, when Poles working abroad return to their families to meet, feast, ski and pray, the exchange rate goes down. 99

building sites abroad are brought home to rebuild the private and public infrastructure. Individual countries view this as an opportunity or a threat, depending on how realistic they are about their own skills' shortages. Cause or effect, the countries that slammed their doors shut to the Poles are not doing as well economically as those who welcomed them.

Guesstimates place between one and two million of the workforce outside the country. Real figures are probably lower but, however many, the effect on the national economy is undeniable. At Christmas, when Poles working abroad return to their families to meet, feast, ski and pray, the exchange rate goes down.

77

Banking

Credit, as in borrowing, is a relatively new sport in Poland but one that Poles have taken to like ducks to water, as a recent aphorism shows: 'If I didn't have so many debts, I wouldn't have anything.' However, debt, both national and personal, still has some way to go before it catches up with the West. In some things, it transpires, it pays to be backward.

The work ethic

The Poles, young and old, do not like to be seen at sweaty toil, especially by outsiders. It lacks style. Work should take place between consulting adults in private.

> **The Poles, young and old, do not like to be seen at sweaty toil, especially by outsiders. It lacks style.**

However, they always were and still are a hard-working bunch. Although state employees might still get away with it, private employers won't tolerate the previously common practice of employees clocking in at their offices but working on commissions for others, so many Poles practise serial employment, racing from one job to another. Then they come home and collapse in a heap in front of the television.

Of course, the tenets of work ethics do not apply to officialdom. As far as the bureaucrat is concerned, papers have to ripen on desks for the prescribed amount of time before they can be looked at, let alone seen to. Where advice for Poles wanting to settle in the UK fits into a two page leaflet, advice on the official requirements facing 'returning' Poles runs to over 50 pages.

Obliging optimists by nature, the Poles want to tell you what they think you want to hear, a fact that is particularly true for estimates of time. Best, therefore, to add anything from five minutes to eternity to the kick off time you are given for social gatherings. It's not that Poles mean to be late, it is just that time's wingèd chariot often overtakes them. This does not apply to work where clockwatching is obligatory, business appointments are kept to the second, and latecomers are told what is thought of them.

> **Obliging optimists by nature, the Poles want to tell you what they think you want to hear, a fact that is particularly true for estimates of time.**

Polish women have long been educated alongside men, and there are as many women as men in engineering and the sciences. There are also plenty of women in the upper reaches of most professions, but those dominated by women – for example, teaching, librarianship and nursing – are poorly paid. Two wages have long been economically essential, and as well as going out to work, women still carry the major burden of housework and childcare. Some things are truly universal.

Job hunting

Jobs in Poland are usually acquired through an elaborate form of patronage. Young people finishing their education scrabble around among relatives and friends aiming to get appointed as supernumerary menials, to be promoted from within if they are any good. Most organisations have room for supernumeraries since many employees are on sabbaticals abroad, so this presents no problems.

> **When Poles tell you how much they earn, they are trying to impress you with the paltriness of their earnings.**

For those left out of this mad form of musical chairs, there is the unemployment office which has a corner dedicated to adverts and the odd advisor. Or they can always emigrate...

Pay

When Poles tell you how much they earn, they give their basic salary, rounded down after deductions. They are trying to impress you with the paltriness of their earnings. When Americans and Western Europeans do the same, they will quote gross figures, rounded up, to show how well they are doing. This may, in part, account for the Polish belief in the overwhelming wealth of all Westerners.

Any conversation on the subject of salaries soon degenerates into an absurd attempt to represent comparative wages by the numbers of bottles of vodka or loaves of bread and fishes the average road-sweeper can buy in a month.

Government

Generations of Poles were told by their conquerors that they were too inept at politics to be trusted with their own self-governance – the 'It's for your own good' excuse for invasion. To ensure they were not infected by foolish ideas of independence, Western borders were also slammed shut, but in vain, as this purported conversation between a Polish president and a favoured actress shows:

'Ask for anything and it's yours.'

'Give passports to everyone who wants to leave.'

'You flirt, you want to be alone with me.'

Nonetheless, over time, the grain of truth contained within the specious argument metamorphosed into a seed of doubt which sprouted into received wisdom. The many years of occupation by one invader or another etched self-doubt into the national character, making gloom the default setting of the Polish psyche. Deep down, Poles fear that they are no good at governing themselves. Thus they are convinced that their government is more corrupt than anyone else's, their politicians more inept, their national scandals beyond the pale and their economy beyond redemption. Although grateful that the crass idiots in power are, for a change, their own crass idiots, criticising the powers-that-be is de rigueur. Poles cannot believe that their government is making anything but a mess of it. It's what governments do.

Thus, the world recession of the last few years, which Poland has weathered comparatively unscathed – the only European country to avoid recession – instead of making the Poles proud, has made them bewildered and deeply depressed. They talk down all indications that Poland is doing well, ignore articles of praise in the world press and disbelieve published statistics. Many are convinced that there is an international conspiracy to keep the bad news about the perilous state of their economy from them.

> **Poles are grateful that the crass idiots in power are, for a change, their own crass idiots.**

Statistical indices (unemployment, production, exports, etc.) show a downturn in the Polish economy and are, therefore, cheering up Poles no end. Their joy is marred only by the fact that the rest of the world is doing even worse. The Polish temperament is geared to surviving bad times. Poles take good news very badly.

Politics

Following the advice of leading Western specialists, Poland opted for proportional representation, a system that is labyrinthine in its complexity, expensive to administer, and inconclusive, virtually guaranteeing hung or minority governments. Then they gave the president powers of veto over legislation. Thus political life became one mad whirl of coalitions, partings, and makings-up, like a mad gavotte with the dancers having to improvise the steps. One cabinet reshuffle was described in the press as 'one new minister and five used ones'.

This reached a crescendo under the Law and Justice Party. These 'Little Polanders' threw invective around so energetically at home and abroad that the Poles began to

> **After Communism, the Poles wanted their government to be perfect and much time and hot air was expended in pursuit of this ideal.**

fear for the reputation of their country and voted for the middle-of-the-road Civic Platform Party who managed to repair the damage the previous xenophobic administration had wrought amongst Poland's neighbours and steered the country into comparatively calm waters. Initially keen on the EU and the euro, economic shenanigans in the region have made the government cautious, which is just as well, as the average Pole's admiration of the EU and the euro have also, unsurprisingly, waned.

After Communism, the Poles wanted their government to be perfect and much time and hot air was expended in pursuit of this ideal. Few perfectionists remain and a new pragmatism prevails. The political pyrotechnics have cooled. All they want now is rulers whose greed or ineptitude are not so great that they bankrupt the nation.

Poles take life's changes gloomily but stoically. The old adage that ran: 'We survived capitalism, we'll out-live communism', now in reverse order, coupled with a wry shrug, seems to be a serviceable enough philosophy. It was a graffiti writer who best encapsulated the Polish attitude towards politicians. Under a sign in the Gents saying 'Hooks for Members of Parliament', he had added 'or their coats'.

Language

Anyone who tells you that the Polish alphabet consists of 's' and 'z' is exaggerating. Only half of it does.

> **66 Anyone who tells you that the Polish alphabet consists of 's' and 'z' is exaggerating. Only half of it does. 99**

Some 'z's are not zeds at all but conjunct consonants, like 'sz' or 'cz', pronounced as 'sh' and 'ch' – sounds that resemble a saw slicing through a nail. Three 's' sounds exist – 's' as in 's' and 'ś' as in 'sh' and 'sz' – like bumble bees in bottles. And then there are three distinct 'c's.

A dot over a 'z' (ż), or a conjunct 'rz', make another unique Polish sound, like a jet aeroplane taking off.

Other letters created to confuse the unwary are 'w' pronounced 'v' and a crossed 'l', (ł), pronounced 'w'. There is also a range of dots, cedillas and diacritics – without which Polish looks naked to a Pole.

There are reported cases of foreigners managing to pronounce Polish words, but not many.

Teach yourself

Should you ever express a willingness to learn the language, most Poles will be only too happy to oblige. What they will try to teach you, if you are not careful, is '*Chrząszcz brzmi w trzcinie*' ('a bug is buzzing in the reeds'), reckoned to be the most difficult phrase an English-speaking tongue could pronounce, until it was ousted by a Czech phrase of even less vowels. A joke has it that a Polish immigrant applying for a driver's licence, has to take an eye test. 'Can you read this?' the examiner asks, holding up:

C Z J W I Z N O S T A C Z

'Read it?' the Pole replies, 'I know the man.'

Inflections and Diminutives

Polish is a highly inflected language: everything declines and conjugates, even more than in Latin. It could be worse: Old Polish had three numbers – single, for one of you, plural for lots, and dual for cosy tête-à-têtes. It is now found only in the sorts of

85

obscure old adages that are best left alone.

One of the spin-offs of inflecting everything is that the order of words is not important – much like the bouffant hair-do, it takes hours to get into place, but once assembled it will take a hurricane to dislodge it. You sort out what is done to whom and why from the case endings. This goes some way to explain the curious order of words pronounced by Poles struggling with the English language and may also explain why, among the groups of immigrants to the United States, they were considered to be slow on the uptake by the others (and thus the butt of endless jokes).

> **Poles professing to be 'charming' or 'exciting' are not being impossibly vain, they're just mixing up their active and passive participles.**

Before you accept some outrageous statement of the 'man bites dog' variety, check if that is really what is meant. It could just be a grammatical misunderstanding and not the sensational piece of gossip you thought it was. Those Poles professing to be 'charming' or 'exciting' are not being impossibly vain, they are just mixing up their active and passive participles.

Where once the Poles would accept no-one's word for anything, the young now take the English words for everything, much to the disgust of the not-so-young. Battle-lines are drawn and skirmishes have commenced over such vile imports as 'hamburger' or 'leasing'. But a language that doesn't even have a word for 'filing' or 'sitcom' is fighting a losing battle.

The Poles miniaturise everything and everyone. Every noun, proper or improper, has a diminutive. A cat that is just called a *kot*, rather than *kotek, koteczek, kicia* or *kiciunia*, is a very large cat indeed. A *maleńki stoliczek* expresses five degrees of diminution: *mały* means little; *maleńki* – very little; *stół* is a table; *stolik* – little table; *stoliczek* – very little table. And yet a *malenki stoliczek* is not as small as all that. That would be *maluteńki stoliczek* (teeny weeny table).

Diminutised, all male names seem to end in -ek and female ones in -sia, regardless of how they started off. Małgorzata (Margaret) thus becomes Małgosia, and is

> **Diminutised, all male names seem to end in -ek and most female ones in -sia, regardless of how they started off.**

usually known as Gosia, Basia is short for Barbara and Kasia is short for Katarzyna (Catherine). Try calling all the women Ania and all men Krzyś (i.e., Krzysztof – Christopher). You will have a 50/50 chance of success, although increasing numbers of infants are now labouring under improbable and unslavonic names such as Damianek, Marlenka or Waneska (Damian, Marlene and Vanessa). After a round of vodka you don't stand an earthly chance, so if all else fails, remember that most Poles are used to being addressed by foreigners as 'Erm...?' and will magnanimously award you points for trying.

The Author

The Lipniackis arrived in Britain (via Kazakhstan and Palestine) when Ewa was three. Educated in a Polish convent boarding school in Northamptonshire, she went so far as to take a degree in Polish at London University.

In her late teens she was one of the first English Poles to set out to rediscover the real Poland, and found a vast family stretching from the Wołomin Poles to the Poles of Częstochowa. She has been extending this family web ever since and supplementing it with a network of friends.

A naturalised Willesden Pole, she maintains close links with the Birmingham, Wolverhampton, Rugby and Galashiels Poles. Her home has become a central node on the Polish world trade routes linking the Warsaw, Kraków, Poznań and Gdańsk Poles with the New York, Toronto, Melbourne, Venezuelan and Brazilian Poles. Like bindweed, Polish roots are long and indestructible.

A librarian by profession, she has written several rarefied works on librarianship and a clutch of children's picture books – most of which are illustrated by her cousin, a Balham Pole.

Xenophobe's® guides

Available as printed books and e-books:

The Americans	The Kiwis
The Aussies	The Norwegians
The Austrians	The Poles
The Belgians	The Portuguese
The Canadians	The Russians
The Chinese	The Scots
The Czechs	The Spanish
The Danes	The Swedes
The Dutch	The Swiss
The English	The Welsh
The Estonians	
The Finns	
The French	
The Germans	Xenophobe's® lingo learners
The Greeks	
The Icelanders	French
The Irish	German
The Israelis	Greek
The Italians	Italian
The Japanese	Spanish

Xenophobe's Guides

The French

French politicians look smart because power itself is chic, attractive, seductive, and one should dress to look the part. The French electorate would never allow any government to intervene in their lives if it were shabbily dressed.

The Germans

Germans love to point out to you what you are doing wrong or what you are failing to do right. Thinking of sneaking through a red light? Don't do it. A hundred Germans will helpfully call out that This Is Not Allowed.

The Americans

Winning is central to the American psyche. As American football coach Vince Lombard put it, 'Winning isn't everything. It's the only thing.' Virtually every event in American life, from school graduation to marriage to buying an automobile, is structured so that one party wins.

The Canadians

Canadians wear an austere smile in the face of adversity, and have a 'grin and bear it' mentality, even if the grin is frozen on their faces by the cold. They like to think that extreme weather conditions build character.

The Italians

Italians grow up knowing that they have to be economical with the truth. All other Italians are, so if they didn't play the game they would be at a serious disadvantage. They have to fabricate to keep one step ahead.

The English

The English share a dislike of anyone behaving in a manner that 'goes too far'. The admired way to behave in almost all situations is to display a languid indifference. Even in affairs of the heart, it is considered unseemly to show too much enthusiasm.

Xenophobe's® Guides are available as e-books from Amazon, iBookstore, and other online sources, and via:

www.xenophobes.com

Xenophobe's® Guides print versions can be purchased through online retailers (Amazon, etc.) or via our web site:

www.xenophobes.com

In the US contact:
IPG Trafalgar Square, Chicago

toll free no: 1-800-888-4741
e-mail: orders@ipgbook.com

In the UK, contact Xenophobe's® Guides

telephone: +44 (0)20 7733 8585
e-mail: info@xenophobes.com

Xenophobe's® Guides
5 St John's Buildings
Canterbury Crescent
London SW9 7QH

Payment can be made with Visa or Mastercard. Postage and packing is FREE in the UK on orders of more than one book (to one address).

Xenophobe's Guides